Leadership Coaching

101 Strategies for the Coach and the Coaching Client to Becoming a True Leader

by Randy Wayne

© **Copyright 2016 by Randy Wayne**
- All rights reserved.

This document is geared towards providing exact and reliable information in regards to the topic and issue covered. The publication is sold with the idea that the publisher is not required to render accounting, officially permitted, or otherwise, qualified services. If advice is necessary, legal or professional, a practiced individual in the profession should be ordered.

- From a Declaration of Principles which was accepted and approved equally by a Committee of the American Bar Association and a Committee of Publishers and Associations.

In no way is it legal to reproduce, duplicate, or transmit any part of this document in either electronic means or in printed format. Recording of this publication is strictly prohibited and any storage of this document is not allowed unless with written permission from the publisher. All rights reserved.

The information provided herein is stated to be truthful and consistent, in that any liability, in terms of inattention or otherwise, by any usage or abuse of any policies, processes, or directions contained within is the solitary and utter responsibility of the recipient reader. Under no circumstances will any legal responsibility or blame be held against the publisher for any reparation, damages, or monetary loss due to the information herein, either directly or indirectly.

Respective authors own all copyrights not held by the publisher.

The information herein is offered for informational purposes solely, and is universal as so. The presentation of the information is without contract or any type of guarantee assurance.

The trademarks that are used are without any consent, and the publication of the trademark is without permission or backing by the trademark owner. All trademarks and brands within this book are for clarifying purposes only and are the owned by the owners themselves, not affiliated with this document.

Disclaimer

Some of the links in this book may be affiliate links. If you click on them and decide to buy something, I may or may not get paid a commission. This doesn't mean that it will cost you extra money. I only include links to products or services that I think are valuable or I use myself.

Table of Contents

INTRODUCTION -- **6**

The Surprising Truth About Leadership ---------------------- 6
A Peculiar Story of Failed Leadership ---------------------- 6
Two Twists of Fate and One Giant Mistake ---------------- 8
The Essence of Leadership ---------------------------------- 12

CHAPTER 1: -- **14**

Creating a Vision and the Law of Attraction ---------------- 14
Manifesting Your Singleness of Purpose ---------------- 20
One Word for All Your Vision ------------------------------ 21

CHAPTER 2 -- **25**

The 29 Universal Skills of Leadership ---------------------- 25

CHAPTER 3 -- **36**

The 18 Skills for Coaching Yourself ------------------------ 36

CHAPTER 4 -- **44**

Coaching Your Clients / 54 Tips on Coaching Your Clients -- 44

CONCLUSION -- **58**

Putting it All Together / ---------------------------------- 58

Creating Visionary Leadership ------------------------------ 58

INTRODUCTION

The Surprising Truth About Leadership

"If your actions inspire others to dream more, learn more, do more and become more, you are a leader."

John Quincy Adams

A Peculiar Story of Failed Leadership

Here is a story of failed leadership. The mid-19th century was an exhilarating time in America, most of the country was experiencing unprecedented growth, cities were drawing strong waves of rural workers, new technologies such as the steam engine, the telegraph, and the internal combustion engine. Tens of thousands of eager and industrious immigrants were streaming into urban areas that were becoming strongholds of manufacturing productivity. Historians have noted that despite a decided lack of institutions, organizations, and corporate traditions, the young capitalist country took advantage of its rich collection of resources to bring out the best new ideas from bright and inventive minds.

However, there was a dark side to much of this economic production. The US was still transitioning out of a slave-based economy that stubbornly refused to shed the moral bankruptcy of the human-chattel ownership, burgeoning city centers were ill-equipped to absorb the great migrations of Irish, German, Polish, and other European groups. But most importantly, rampant human exploitation became the norm even as brilliant inventions were developed to actually improve the human condition. In the midst of all this chaos and great possibility, a person of genius, vision, and leadership could make and indelible mark on the future of the country.

In 1866, a young man named Tom arrived from Michigan to Louisville, Kentucky to begin work as telegraph operator for the respected communications company, Western Union. He was a bright and curious kid, barely 19 years of age, but had, through a series of twists and turns landed a respectable job despite several early harbingers of a less than fortunate life.

As a young boy, he was raised by a family of modest means living in the port city of Milan, Ohio. He was always known as a rambunctious and active child that could not, and would not sit still---a true terror to his teachers. He constantly and relentlessly asked questions, some of them bordering on impertinence, and he possessed an insatiable inquisitiveness. Tom made few friends---a fact that was exacerbated by the fact the boy was born with an unusually broad forehead. The effect of having a larger than average head size combined with the constant questioning he asked of the adults around him eventually exhausted their patience.

Only his mother recognized that her little boy was not being disrespectful nor willful, but rather, he was extraordinary bright, and more than likely a bit bored from the tedium of schooling imparted on so many youths at that time. She saw his potential and proceeded to develop her on curriculum to channel his passions and voracious curiosity. In effect, she was his coach---guiding him, giving him feedback on his studies, correcting him, and helping him harness his abilities and encouraged his curiosity.

Her decision to provide Tom with as structured and rigorous a home-school education as she could, rather than giving up on him, played a critical role in developing his sense of perseverance and fierce independence—two qualities that served him well when the first of two remarkable events that would change the course of his life forever occurred.

Two Twists of Fate and One Giant Mistake

First, when Tom was 14, he was riding a train when he noticed that a young boy of 3 had wandered unattended onto the path of an oncoming boxcar. Before he could think of it, the teenager scooped the bewildered child up and rolled away from certain injury or death. Within moments, the boys frantic father rushed forward and gratefully embraced his little boy. In a gesture of profound thankfulness, the man revealed that he was no just another passenger, but was the station agent for that train depot and insisted that the young Tom be trained by himself personally to become a telegraph operator.

This vocation was a significant educational advancement, but more importantly, being a telegraph operator meant being on the cusp of 19th century innovation. During the next few years, Tom quickly mastered not only the fundamentals of the telegraph system but specifically requested to work during the late shift so that he could perform his own personal experiments with the leftover equipment in peace and quiet. His fascination with this so-called burgeoning "communication science" became the center-point in his life as he transferred to work in different cities from the South into the Northeast. Despite his valuable expertise, Tom's initial projects regarding his various inventions met with limited success. He was often under-employed, poor, and constantly on the road to look for new work and capital opportunities to fund his rapidly refined, technologically advanced projects.

Having reached his middle 20s in dire straits, Tom set forth for New York, living little better than a street beggar until the second of extraordinary twists of fate befell him. For quite a number of days, Tom had found a way to sleep in the basement of one of the many buildings situated in New York's awe-inspiring financial district. Having emerged in a stupor one morning, and just after begging for a cup of tea from a kindly street vendor, he noticed there was ruckus on the street. It turned out that the manager of that buildings brokerage firm was in a state of panic over a stock-ticker machine in the building that had stopped working, refusing to print out quotes. For any brokerage firm, this was an all-out disaster as it effectively halted all trading. Tom quickly offered his services and within a short period of time, not only quickly diagnosed the broken gear within the system but rigged it to work again.

It is this eerie repeat of the event nearly 10 years ago, when he first saved the little boy, that Tom was rewarded richly for his quick thinking and nimbleness. He averted disaster, and the manager of the brokerage firm promptly offered him a position to repair all defective machines in the building. This arrival of a steady and well-paying job offered the required stability and financial capital that gave Thomas Alva Edison the pathway to build precisely the inventions he wanted.

Within a few short years, and before he turned 30, Edison would develop a world-class laboratory and move his operations to New Jersey, where he would work for the rest of his life, introducing the world a series of ingenious, and now indispensable inventions: the phonograph, dozens of original designs and improvements on the telegraph, culminating in the telephone, and of course—the electric light. His works were so marvelous in design and execution that crowds of people would flock to witness his various scientific demonstrations in slack-jawed admiration. Over time, this ability to create seemingly magical results from the cutting edge of scientific discovery paved the way for Edison to be given the strikingly fitting nickname, "The Wizard of Menlo Park." But how can Thomas A. Edison, one of the greatest inventors of the 19th and 20th centuries, also be known as a failed leader?

Edison was not quite 40 years old when he meets Nikola Tesla, a 6 foot 4-inch Serbian immigrant who arrived with a formal European education and a nearly unknown reputation. But what the young engineering genius possessed was a letter of introduction from Edison's business colleagues, Charles Batchelor. In that letter he noted that, "I know two great men, and you are one of them. The other is this young man!"

At this midway point in his life (Edison would live to over 80 years), the older inventor was much revered as a living legend. He could have stopped his work entirely, never producing another invention or filed one more patent, and still be considered one of the most successful entrepreneurs of the 19th century. Yet it is at this critical juncture that Edison makes a disastrous misstep.

Looking Tesla up and down, Edison immediately recognized the natural brilliance of the awkward and gangly immigrant-inventor in front of him, but he was highly contemptuous of Tesla's development of an alternating current (AC) system. He didn't see that the more versatile AC system was far superior in conduction, safety, and reliability than the direct current (DC) model. Edison fought fiercely for direct current, which he harnessed to illuminate New York City in 1882. Having made his fame, fortune, and reputation on DC, Edison stubbornly believed that there could never be any discernable improvement on what he already established.

Soon, the venerable older genius fought a vicious multi-year war of attrition to crush Tesla's campaign to move toward the AC system. Not only did Edison fail to recognize that the majority of major urban areas that had at first adopted electrical grids were already rapidly outgrowing his original power systems, he actively launched attacks to take down Tesla, who by then, had left his mentor (who had refused to pay him for his work), to work with George Westinghouse, a visionary entrepreneur who saw the great potential of Tesla's AC model---a technology that we use today to power small lights as well as large industrial machines across great distances.

Today, Edison remains an American icon, but with his stubborn preoccupation with discrediting Tesla and his outright rejection of what was clearly the superior advancement, he never went on to summon up his previous levels of remarkably original innovation. In the second half of his life, Edison spent his time filing patents that were improvements on items he already established, or minor products. He refused to listen to colleagues and business partners. After declining to embrace the new era of AC, the famously persistent inventor poured all of his hopes and resources into another ill-advised scheme to use magnetic technology to derive iron from ore; a time-wasting catastrophe that nearly closed down his laboratory imperiled the careers of his research staff that worked for him.

Toward the end of his life, his biggest investors, such as JP Morgan, who had championed him throughout much of his career, realized the limitations of Edison's remarkable stubbornness. When Edison was able to channel his relentless doggedness toward difficult but ingenious projects, the inventor could literally illuminate a dark world and bring astonishment and delight to the masses. But it is Edison's failure to be open-minded and flexible, his refusal in exercising humility, ultimately lead to a total and complete lapse in much needed leadership.

Tesla, on the other hand, reportedly loved giving his imagination free reign rather than let it rigidly define the world around him. By his own account, his inventions existed whole and complete in his mind before he physically created them in his laboratory. He truly believed in the "magic" of science.

The Essence of Leadership

What can be learned from the experience of Edison and Tesla? Both were genius inventors, both worked very hard to develop their projects, both are considered leaders and giants of scientific advancement today. However, it is only Tesla that would go on to truly harness the power of his imagination to push past the rigid thinking traps that Edison allowed his mind to fall into. No doubt, both men had visions of great technologies but only one of them was truly visionary when it came to leadership.

This book is about developing the skills of leadership to inspire yourself and others to be their best and reach their highest personal potential. Whether you are an already established individual who has seen a great deal of leadership success already in your life, or someone who is getting back on their feet after some major setbacks in your family or career, or somewhere in-between, where you feel you are doing "fine" but want to learn new strategies to become a breakout leader in all of your personal and professional relationships.

This book focuses on the <u>essence of leadership</u>: the development of thinking in the highest frame of mind such that it will bring to you the success you desire and deserve.

Who should read this book?

- ☐ If you are a person who wants to know the general skills of leadership.

- ☐ If you are a coach who wants some advanced strategies for himself or herself.

- ☐ If you are a coach who is looking for strategies for his or her client on how to become better leaders.

You will learn 101 strategies and techniques to reach your creative potential whether it is for yourself or for others. This book also focusses on the model of coaching as a special form of leadership. The qualities of a world-class coach can be applied to all industries, professions, and settings. You will see how you yourself can apply the leadership principles of coaching to bring great joy and success. But before we look at the art and craft of leadership coaching, the first chapter will talk about a core theme that underscores success overall—the law of attraction.

Good luck in your journey toward manifesting all your most dearly held desires and dreams!

CHAPTER 1:

Creating a Vision and the Law of Attraction

"Create the highest, grandest vision possible for your life, because you become what you believe."

Oprah Winfrey

Vince Lombardi once said that, "Success demands singleness of purpose." In those five words, Lombardi, one of football's most beloved coaches, captures the most important lesson of leadership success---in order to achieve what you want, stay ruthlessly focused on the one essential thing that makes all the difference.

There is no room for the clutter of random goals, ideas, and half-hearted devotions. Find the one thing, the big vision, and resolve to focus on that.

Think about it, have you ever had one of those days that ran on endless multi-tasking? You wake up in the morning and begin doing several things at once, like eating breakfast, getting dressed, finding your keys, packing your briefcase, filling up your kids' backpacks, and maybe even cleaning up, making your bed, and brushing your teeth! And once you get to work, the endless juggling does not stop as you rush about attending meetings, answering emails, listening in on conference calls, or physically cleaning up. By the end of the day, even if you've moved forward in whittling down your to-do list, how do you feel? Exhausted? Frustrated? Confused on what the next thing to do might be? Wondering perhaps, why you are still on this endless treadmill of ticking items off your to-do list, but never feeling that you quite accomplished enough?

This is an entirely frustrating and futile condition. Research has shown that multi-tasking is ironically, once of the most inefficient, and LEAST effective modes that a human being can experience. It may seem like you are getting a ton of stuff done, but in actuality, your brain is not simply wired in a manner that makes doing many things at once truly possible. For starters, you actually aren't doing several tasks at one time. Instead, you are performing only one task at a time---the full capacity of your cognitive capacity.

Take for example, a task that people often perform not on its own, but usually in conjunction with something else, such as talking on the phone. You are chatting away while you are listening to the television news in the background, thinking that you are performing both equally well. Meanwhile, your brain is on quite a roller coaster ride without your knowledge. The human mind is actually only attending to one thing at a time---you are either talking to your friend, or you are actively taking in the news—not both at the same time. The actual activity your brain performs is that it toggles back and forth, switching gears, so to speak as you listen to your friend talk for a few minutes, then let your eyes and ears roam toward the TV. It may seem that you are doing both at once, but basically, your attention is pulled in so many different directions that you are more accurately *task-switching rather* than multi-tasking.

Consider how inefficient this is---you are wasting valuable time switching from one task to the other. And each time your attention volleys from one thing to another, you lose precious time getting readjusted. The lesson here is clear, dive deep, stay deep, and finish that one thing. And in terms of leadership, you must have one singular vision.

In this chapter, you will be asked to perform a writing exercise that will help you clarify your singular purpose. All you need is a pen, some paper, and some quite uninterrupted time of 25 minutes. This is not a long exercise, but it does ask a lot of you---it asks that you be utterly honest with yourself. Do not skip this exercise, even if you feel like you've done some form of journaling, writing, or reflection on dreams and goals before. Performing the writing exercise is critically important because they are fundamental building blocks of leadership coaching. So, grab your pen and paper, take a seat, and you'll begin the writing in just a minute.

After your writing exercise is complete, you'll be introduced to 29 of the best strategies for successful leadership coaching. Whether you want to coach just yourself, or others, you will find that these 29 tips apply to every person, every time.

How do I Create A Leadership Vision?

Let's make something very clear, a singular vision like the one advocated by Lombardi does not mean that only ONE goal, or ONE dream, or ONE idea is all you can have on your plate at one time. Singleness of purpose can also speak to a powerful, transformative image in your minds-eye that encompasses everything at one time. In order to craft that particular vision, begin with clarifying exactly what it is you want in your life. The following writing exercise will help being your journey toward articulating what you've been dreaming about.

First, sit with your pen and paper, and imagine the following scene: you are walking along the street one day, on your lunch break. Instead of going to pick up something quick at a restaurant, or eat at your desk, you decide to take a stroll—you feel more restless than hungry, apparently. For months, you've been feeling agitated, some of the reasons are obvious, you wish you could lose some weight, other reasons you can't quite describe.

But you know that you can't keep waking up each morning, wondering why you don't feel as excited as you'd like. You feel unsure and unhappy. You don't know what you want. And, to be sure, you aren't the type of person who believes that all negative emotions are bad---there is no denying that sadness, anger, and loneliness have a role in the human condition. But you would like to find a sense of purpose for your life.

Suddenly, across the street, you see someone who looks familiar. In fact, this person looks exactly like someone you know very, very well. You rush across the street, suddenly overcome with the urge to scream in order to get their attention, and in fact you do yell, as you start to break out in a full-on run toward them, frantically waving your arms. You feel in that moment, that you absolutely must get this person's attention. At the sound of your raised voice, this eerily familiar person turns their face toward you---a face you realize that you know intimately because...it is your face.

As you come to screeching halt right in front of this person, it dawns on you in absolute wonder that this person, standing there so casually, and unsurprised by your presence, does not simply resemble you; it goes beyond the type of striking similarity that people say their doppelgangers possess---this person IS you. The two of you have the same hands, the same eye shape and color, the same slight bow to your legs, and you both have the same down to the tiny mole on the left side of your chin, right below the corner of your lip. You stand looking at each other, exactly the same except for one astonishing difference. This person is at least 20 years older than you are right in that moment. The person who is you gets right down to the point:

"I'm here to help you change your life...if you want that." You stand there, looking at yourself. Then, you notice it, this particular "you" has more wrinkles, their shoulders are slightly more stooped, and then your gaze travels up to the gray hair. You stand there in stupefied shock, so flabbergasted you can barely move.

This person smiles at you and states calmly, as if your meeting was the most natural thing in the world, "You have one minute to ask me one question about yourself. Looking at me, you can tell that I know more about how your life has turned out than you do in this moment, and I can tell you anything you want about how your life is based on how you are living now. And, I can also tell you what your life is like if you change your life. I know it all and everything as it pertains to you, what you did, what you will do, and how it all turns out—I know all the scenarios. You can ask me anything you wish."

The figure goes on to tell you that their powers are limited, that there are some boundaries to their omniscient knowledge. They tell you that they have no knowledge of things like the direction of major political events in the future, nor can they name for you any winning lottery numbers. In short, they only know certain things, and that knowledge is solely about you, well, that is, the "future you" from an all-seeing vantage point.

You are allowed to ask one question only. What do you ask your future self?

Write down that one question on a piece of paper. Take a look at your question. Here are some examples of what you might ask: "How did my plan to write and publish my novel work out for me?" or "Did I become CEO of the company after all?" or "How many children do I have in the future?"

Chances are, the subject of your question can be boiled down to a few key words in content and in the emotions they evoke. Try to find the common idea or topic behind your question. Here's an example, let's say your question is this: "Am I divorced from my spouse?" The fact that you have allotted your one and only question to this subject effectively pinpoints the main cause of your concern in this moment...your marriage. Perhaps you and your spouse are experiencing some marital troubles at this time? Have things been difficult lately? Write down all your thoughts surrounding this question and what significance that question possesses for you regarding your emotional wellbeing.

Remember to not stay trapped inside the literal meanings of the words that come to mind, as you continue exploring the question, ask yourself what are the thoughts associated with the question? You may find that what is actually weighing on your mind is not only about the state of your future marriage, but the topic of love in general, or how you desire but feel unable to attain healthy relationships. You may also find that you have been troubled with feelings of insecurity about your family overall. It is up to you to write continuously until you feel you have gotten it "all out of your system" using the one question you asked as a catalyst to explore the depths of your psyche.

The more you reflect on this singular question that you ask your future self, you will begin to see a larger picture---a picture that reflects what you truly want your ideal future to look like. Perhaps you long for marital harmony, explore what this might look like? Is it a new home that you and your spouse just purchased because you final had enough money to buy your dream home? Or do you see the two of you on a beach as much in love as ever before? This vision of how your life is being lived is entirely from your imagination. Describe it detail, and write about how this imagery makes you feel. This beautiful picture speaks to your deepest desires. This is your "singleness" of purpose.

Manifesting Your Singleness of Purpose

Now that you have thoroughly explored your one question, try to distill your image into one paragraph. In just a few sentences, try to capture exactly what you would like to see happen. In this case, you can write something like this:

"I envision that my spouse and I are sitting quietly in front of a fireplace at the end of a long day. It is unusually cold outside, so we are happy to feel safe and warm inside. The kids are upstairs after getting a chance to play all day in the snow. Both of us was able to enjoy this vacation because I've gotten a much better job recently where I work less hours doing something I love. We talk about renovating the kitchen and plan a family reunion in the spring. I feel secure, happy, and joyful that we are together."

Once you have this paragraph written (and perhaps re-written until it feels like you have fully captured what you are wanting to experience in your life), *create one sentence* from the paragraph. This summarizing into one substantive sentence helps you to further narrow down your intention. Write your sentence in the present tense, as if you are experiencing the image right then and there. An example of making one sentence from the imaginative paragraph above may look like this:

"I am living in such harmony with my spouse and our children where we spend time together being a relaxed and loving family."

By the time you write this sentence, you'll begin to automatically see the visual images that accompany the paragraph earlier. With each time you interact with the vision, it deepens in complexity and conviction in your mind's eye.

Finally, after you've thoroughly explored your question, crafted a detailed paragraph, and then condensed your singleness of vision down to one sentence, it is now time to go one final step---decide on one word to evoke everything you are asking to receive.

One Word for All Your Vision

This is the most concentrated form of your vision. There is no more material left to condense, and you are left with the ultimate singleness of purpose. Most people may think this is an overly simplistic idea, and that such brevity would not only end up being forgotten, but useless. After all, it's just one word, what can one word accomplish?

Well, as it turns out, a lot can happen with just one word. Read each of the following words as you would an entire sentence. Say the word out loud and pause to really hear yourself say it:

- Breath.
- Love.
- Kind.
- Career.
- Healthy.
- Forever.

Child.

Fire.

Inspire.

How does each word make you feel? Every word has a powerful impact in the mind of the person who utters it. This one word doesn't have to mean anything to everyone, it just *has to mean something specific for you.* Reducing your vision to a well-chosen word loads it with a great deal of power. You will feel the word and its meaning in your body. In this case, the one sentence offers up several excellent choices for the one word---and some will happen within the sentence itself, for example: "Harmony" or "Family" or even "Love." And the word could simply show up where it has not shown up before, yet somehow, the word feels appropriate and fitting when it occurred to you. This may be something like the word, "Agreement" (meaning that you and your spouse feel so easy and loving together because of your feelings of coordination).

Again, these words may feel generic---but that is only because this example is generic. Once you are free to generate your initial magical question, and then craft your one-sentence from your one descriptive paragraph, the one word may jump out at you as the right word, just for you.

With this one word, you will be able to attract the very thing you have been imagining to yourself. **The Law of Attraction** states that everything that we see in visible universe, was once just a thought in your mind. Consider the story of Nikola Tesla in chapter one. Tesla, you may recall, was in possession of a thriving imagination, he often envisioned entirely elaborate and complex systems solely in his mind before creating them, in exacting detail in his laboratory.

You, too can create wonderful things entirely from your mind, and if you are diligent about holding these images in your head, *with a steady faith in the belief that you already possess them*, it is only a matter of time before they arrive on your doorstep.

Once you realize that everything you've ever really wanted already exists in the real world, but simply needs to be taken out of your mind, then the rest is easy—just call upon your one manifestation word and it will conjure up exactly what you want in your life. This keystone to your deepest dreams doesn't negate hard work---you still have to put in the labor of dutifully working toward your goal. But the difference in having this key word lies in how magically doors will open to you, opportunities will blossom, and a sense that you are already living the magic of your fantasy in the day to day reality of your life.

How is this possible? The Law of Attraction is both elegant in its simplicity but complex in its origins. For the purposes of this book, it is sufficient to say that a variety of new thinking writers, contemporary philosophers, as well as investigators of the metaphysical theories of quantum mechanics have worked to better describe the inner workings of this inscrutable theory. The core idea is that all matter is made up of energy particles that are in constant motion, therefore, all matter is energy, but the range of frequencies fall along a vast spectrum of different attunements.

The saying that "like energy attracts like energy" refers to the tendency for matter to match their vibrations such that the matter becomes "manifest" or somehow "physical" in the world. The Law exists not merely as a theoretical maxim, but may be reliably deployed in a practical manner, such that one may look to the genesis of thought as the first step toward the cultivation of physical matter.

Therefore, if you think something, you generate a cascade of energy emanating from that thought. If that thought is one of "low energy" such as the case with negative emotions (sadness, anger, grief, fear, pensiveness, anxiety), you will attract negative emotions in kind. But if you radiated the positive energy, thoughts, and beliefs that you actually want to feel, then the likelihood that you will attract those visions into your life increases dramatically.

Now that you have been introduced to the radical metaphysical idea surrounding the law of attraction, let's put the theory into practice.

CHAPTER 2

The 29 Universal Skills of Leadership

"Leadership is the capacity to translate vision into reality."

Warren G. Bennis

What does it mean to be a leader in your life? The popular image that comes to mind is someone others consider to be "important" or "powerful" in some way that we find valuable, so that they are given a special platform to speak to and advise others. Leaders are the people who are supposed to stand charismatically at podiums, or on a large glittering stage, to deliver a rousing speech and inspirational calls to action. We think of important political or social authorities, powerful, high status individuals, and celebrities or other eminent people as leaders because they are the ones given the responsibility to command, influence, or manage others.

In reality, true leadership is not only the ability to direct a crowd's attention, but it is also characterized by taking command of a situation that needs direction or improvement. And in that case, leadership exists in a great variety of directions, whether it is being in charge of improving your life, or the life of others. Leadership is taking charge and getting things done.

You are reading this book so you can take charge of your life, achieve your goals, and create the kind of life you want. The following 29 strategies present you with the most fundamental things to know about becoming an assertive and confident leader in all aspects of your personal and professional paths.

Leadership Coaching

Before we introduce them, it is important for you to write down your goals---this should be easy now that you have clarified your one true vision. To break down your vision into actionable goals follow these steps:

- ☐ State your one-word vision.

- ☐ Look over your description of this singular vision and explicitly sate 2-3 ways that you can take a leadership position in changing your current reality into your longed-for vision.

- ☐ For example, if your one-word vision is "Home" then, after consulting your paragraph descriptors, you might end up describing your goals in the following ways:

    - o "I will take charge of letting my wife know I care about her by arranging a fun date night once a week."

    - o "I will take the initiative in sending her favorite bouquet of flowers once a month."

    - o "I will take ownership of my part in the relationship and...."

- ☐ Write each of your goals in this way of positioning yourself as a leader. This will influence the way you see yourself as an empowered individual who can affect change in your life.

Here now, it is time to translate, as Warren Bennis states it so well in the quote that opens this chapter, your "vision into reality" by using leadership. The following 29 tips may be used in any combination or deployed selectively as the situation calls for it. As you start to put your action items into effect, be sure to refer to these strategies as you go along.

1. **Vision:** Whether you call upon the visions associated with your one word (as presented for your practice in the previous chapter) or make it a daily habit to simply visualize the things, people, and situations you really desire, you must continually return to these images to develop command of your life.

2. **Listen:** In order to become a true leader, be a careful listener. It is a sad fact that most people only "hear" the other person long enough so that they can take the signal of when it is their turn to speak. When you truly listen, without speaking, commenting, or monitoring your own thoughts, you would have done something that 90% of others do not do. This makes you an extraordinary outlier in a sea of mediocre human interactions.

3. **Eye Contact:** Hold your eye contact with a person for 3-5 seconds longer than you usually do, research studies have shown that intimacy and rapport is built in the non-threatening gave of another human being. Most people break eye contact to early due to social convention (women are especially pushed to cast their eyes away in a non-challenging manner), but if you soften your gaze while maintaining eye contact, people report feeling happier and more friendly with the person they are looking at.

4. **Intuition:** Listen to your first impressions, thoughts and rumblings in your gut. This does not necessarily require that you act upon those half-formed ideas or feelings, but you must take note of them. Make a

deliberate effort to stop and listen to various sensations in your body and the notions that cross your mind---they provide great clues to better inform your decisions. Great leaders heed these messages, but balance their gut instincts with evidence and common sense.

5. **Compassion:** There will be many times when you feel unsympathetic or unmoved by people who you experience as irritating or annoying. Sometimes you just can't understand why they are the way that they are. But you do not have to accept their behavior nor condone it in order to feel equanimity toward them. This is a great gift to them, that you do not judge them, but an even greater gift to yourself to be compassionate rather than unkind.

6. **Humor:** You don't have to force a joke or be a comedienne, but you can often find something hilarious, weird, or amusing simply by paying attention to the world around you. If you see something funny, share it with another person, this goes a great way toward establishing trust and rapport.

7. **Specific:** Great leaders often have larger than life personas, they are associated with flowery, grandiose speeches, and inspiring calls to action. But in reality, great leadership is the stuff of modest and specific details. That is, a competent leader will provide concrete answers to the questions of who, what, when, where, and why. These are actionable items that bring about real progress---and isn't that the point of following a great leader?

8. **Honesty:** Honesty is an absolute non-negotiable trait for a leader. There are not varying degrees of candor,

there is the truth on one hand, and the non-truth on the other. Within in the bounds of appropriate compassion, speak the truth all the time.

9. **Story:** Today's society is abundantly rich with information, statistics, and the latest scientific research, especially in service to the field of human development and self-improvement. At times, this treasure trove of useful materials can prove overwhelming in its rawest form. The development of story around the data creates a relatable narrative and reaches out to the person listening in a very human and effective way. Try to use the power of story craft to get your point across.

10. **Example:** Like the arc of telling a story (tip #9 above), or similar to tip #7 (be specific) giving examples serves two major purposes, to build a bridge of rapport and excitement to your audience, as well as provide a concrete example of what can and should be done so that the listener is not set adrift in a sea of vague platitudes.

11. **Integrity:** Similar to tip #8 (honesty), possessing integrity is also a non-negotiable and required trait for any good coach or leader. Integrity draws on the old maxim, "do what you said you would do" where the leader follows through on stated calls to action. This uniformity in behavior demonstrates that the leader can be trusted to keep their promises.

12. **Vulnerability:** Too often mistaken for weakness, vulnerability has gotten a bad reputation for being the human quality that allows others to take advantage or exploit a person who dares to exhibit exposed defenselessness. Nothing can be further from the truth.

Admitting that you have made mistakes, or have been susceptible to poor decision making in the past can be repurposed (after your lessons are learned, of course—mistakes must be processed so that you arrive at a greater level of progress, do not present your mistakes as an educational experience if you haven't completed that assignment yet). Create a safe space for you and others to be vulnerable with one another.

13. **Innovation:** What would happen if you started a revolution? Leaders look to advance, improve upon, and re-orientate classic solutions to new problems. They also see the possibility of new solutions to old problems. Innovation requires creativity deployed in service of an already skill set, that is, get good at something, and then get creative with your skills. But most of all, innovation requires courage, so be brave and advance your novel idea!

14. **Consistency:** Unlike integrity, which is defined as keeping your word, or "doing what you said you would do," consistency is about developing a routine that will work for you to most efficiently advance your life. If you go to the gym each and every day, you will quickly find you are stronger and in better shape. Our habits make our lives, so be sure to establish healthy habits. Be consistent in your application of values and principles, as well as in your behaviors. People pay attention to your reliability.

15. **History:** Aside from the tired cliché that those who do not heed history are bound to repeat it, there is the notion of creating and keeping legacy. Truly great leaders will look at their own history and their client's history---what has happened before? What are the

major mistakes? What can be learned? What is worth keeping and preserving? Please note that these are also the questions that can help you hone in on what is your "single mindedness of purpose" when you were performing the vision exercise in the previous chapter.

16. **Plan:** There is no underestimating the power of organization. Having vision, charisma, and drive is one thing, but if you cannot remember if or when you followed-up on that networking meeting for your new career, or if you missed your daughter's science fair because you got caught up in another new project, then you will not get very far on your journey for greater success.

17. **Partner:** Great leaders cannot do everything alone. Your singular vision for the future may be your own, but there are a variety of endless tasks, not to mention challenges and obstacles, that will require that you seek out and create synergy with others. This is not only good advice here, as a strategy to increase your own leadership skills, but is necessary to frame your coaching relationship in this manner so that your client will understand the importance of this strategy.

18. **Language:** How do you use choose your words? Do you use them carelessly without thought? Are you more precise and think before you speak? Do you curse? Do you use colloquialism? Research has shown that individuals are deeply but subtly influenced by language and word choice, and the right word at the right time can make a world of difference in how advice, guidance, and support is needed (and the converse is true---the wrong words at the wrong time may torpedo an otherwise good relationship). Here, it is wise to

listen to the client themselves and see what words, imagery, and metaphor they guide themselves toward.

19. **Resources:** Look around you, what are your resources in terms of expertise, knowledge, materials, that you have at the ready? Taking stock of what you need for your journey to a greater, more fulfilling life will help expedite your adventures. Let's say for example, that you envision learning to horseback ride because you love horses and have always wanted to learn to ride. A question about resources is more about what you need to have rather than just what you need to do. Where are the stables in your area? Who are the best instructors? What equipment do you need to purchase?

20. **Dignity:** There is nothing more inspiring than a person who is following their dreams. At the same time, there is also few things more annoying than someone who talks constantly about their self-improvement schemes. Other people are usually happy for you, but if you tend to then brag, lecture, or impart your new "wisdom" that you've acquired in your everyday conversations, or make unwanted announcements about what you are doing next, that is not exhibiting dignity. Be a model of self-respect and restraint, so that others will be moved by your choices rather than bored or contemptuous.

21. **Excellence:** Whatever you choose to do, do it well. The reason why you have received half-hearted results in the past is likely because of your half-hearted efforts. Pursuing excellence requires a measure of thoughtfulness. What are your core values and beliefs? How do you go about implementing your values throughout your day? How do your choices reflect your

beliefs and so on? Excellence is constant number of choices over time.

22. **Role Model:** Actively cultivating and getting to know role models can offer a world of benefits to your success journey. Find and pursue (respectfully, of course), the people who you wish to emulate. And do not limit yourself to traditional models of success---it is fairly easy to find an example of a successful entrepreneur, or a well-educated person, but do not overlook the especially kind family member who is always a great listener, or the neighbor who exhibited extraordinary courage in their youth. There are many ways to be great, look for role models in all avenues of life you'd like to pursue.

23. **Pay it Forward:** In support of tip #22 (role model), think of yourself as being a role model for others. Leadership requires deliberate mentorship, so seek out new avenues in which you can become useful to others who are often younger or less experienced than you. Likely, these up and coming individual would love the chance to better understand how they might become more like you. There are many opportunities to serve in your community, so look to church groups, worthy nonprofit organizations, and community groups. Performing mentorship to those who really need it can be one of the most rewarding experiences you can have as a leader.

24. **Negotiate:** Good leaders, if they are able to harness the required skills of vision (tip #1), good listening (tip #2), planning (tip #16) and tip #19 (resources), then they are well on their way to being a master negotiator. A good negotiator, contrary to popular belief, is not a

ruthless, unscrupulous deal maker who operates with the sole purpose of getting as much from the other side as they. Instead, truly masterful negotiators have a profound understanding of what the other side truly wants, not so that they can exploit them, but to better give them what they want in balance to their own stated preferences.

25. **Diversity:** Variety is the spice of life. And this adage is useful for all aspects of your life. Be adventurous in your food, but also your friends, meet new people, do new things. Most importantly, learn new things. Yes, the routine of your habits provides you with an anchor for creating sustainable success (do things that bring about good results long enough, and you will receive the results you desire). However, being open to a variety of different experiences creates dynamic tension in your life which leads to greater satisfaction and happiness.

26. **Grit:** Big corporations often spend big bucks to conduct all kinds of personality testing, however, research in the field of industrial and organizational psychology has shown that there are very few characteristics that actually predict how an employee may actually fit into the organization. But most managers do agree, those who show determination and drive to perform their jobs, even when that work is tedious, boring, or unrewarding in the short term, are the most well-liked, respected, and productive colleagues. So, to be a great leader, be persistent, persevere in spite of setbacks, that is, be gritty.

27. **Respect:** This strategy calls for the two-way street component of respect---you must give respect to receive respect. Be a person who treats everyone (and this is

everyone, form the person who serves you food at the restaurant to the CEO of your company) with the same regard and esteem.

28. **Loyalty:** In the same manner that tip #27 above (respect) requires reciprocity (you must be loyal to others in order to receive loyalty) in order to operate. Being loyal to yourself and to others does not mean you blindly support or condone behavior and actions you support---if you cannot defend the value of something or someone you find offensive, it is vital you step away. Loyalty, in this case requires a judicious support of those who have earned such trust and allegiance.

29. **Reflection:** There will be many times when you will become so busy pursuing your dreams and goals that you forget what they were so prized and valued by you. Why work so hard when you have no idea why you are doing so? This strategy involves building in "pause" moments in your pursuit of excellence. Be sure to practice a form of grateful, quite reflection ideally every day. Your mind and body will thank you.

Now that you've been introduced to the most tried and true strategies for becoming a leader in your life, we will now look at strategies that help you cover the role of leadership coaching to enhance your game.

CHAPTER 3

The 18 Skills for Coaching Yourself

"I think the most important thing about coaching is that you have to have a sense of confidence about what you're doing. You have to be a salesman, and you have to get your players, particularly your leaders, to believe in what you're trying to accomplish on the basketball floor."

Phil Jackson

What exactly is coaching? To start with, we need to take a look at the very special role that coaches play in society. Most people are familiar with athletic coaches who work with athletes and sports players of all ages in order to help develop their prowess in that particular game. Coaches are the ones who run you through drills, correct your swing, monitor your improvement, and in general develop your skills in context of the sport.

But what if you consider that life itself is a sport? That there are skills and strategies that life requires of us to "win" at the game of life? If that is the case, then it goes to reason that coaching is a form of hands-on leadership. Where leaders may act as far away or removed figures, coaches have to be right there, close to you and in your space to guide you through to your goals.

Below are 18 tips for how to be your own best coach. Again, like in the previous chapter, you may modify, mix and match, or otherwise create your own coaching profile to best suit your needs.

30. **Simplify:** It really boils down to a simple matter of math. If you find yourself swimming in extra possessions, the overall effect is that you will feel weighted down. Physical objects take up space in your closet and in your head. And the care, cleaning, and storing of them will weight you down. Do yourself a favor and begin looking at your items, one by one. Can you do without that badminton set? Or that extra hope chest, or shoe rack? Do you really need 10 sets of beach towels if you don't live near the beach?

31. **Brainstorm:** It is a shame that brainstorming as a creative, idea-generating exercise is mostly used only in corporate or organizational settings. But the technique can be used every day, and in a very practical manner. To do this, sit or stand near a place where you can write comfortably and at length. Set a timer for 10 minutes and write continuously all that is on your mind about your goal. You may find that during your writing, it turns out that things you were meaning to do are not needed, but instead, you may have an even better idea.

32. **Movement:** Many people dread the idea of exercise, but there is good news---any movement, no matter how small, is simply better than none. That's right, you don't need to run 8 miles a day, or compete in mixed martial arts contest every weekend to reap the benefits of movement. So, go take a walk, stretch, work in the garden, touch your toes, or play a round of golf or tennis. The major benefit here is that it all counts as progress. And the remarkable result will be that once you begin raking up these small victories, you will begin to feel like the bigger challenges are possible to overcome.

33. **Eating:** It's no secret that what you eat has an enormous impact on the day to day quality of your health. The National Consumer Council reported that over half of American adults at any given time are currently on a diet. There is a seemingly endless array of diets and food choices you can make. Which diet is the best one? As cliché as it may sound, the best diet is the diet that works best for you. But making the conscious effort to improve your relationship with food, along with tip #32 on movement, will create the support structure to reach all of your goals.

34. **Get Social:** One of the key ideas behind coaching is that it's the feeling of support and feedback which drives you toward excellence. In order to cultivate this for yourself, as your own coach, you'll need to reach out to others, network, make connections, and in general create for yourself a crowd of people. Getting with others means sparking ideas, getting insight, and most importantly, having fun.

35. **Style:** You are not what you wear. But if what you are wearing is distracting to either you, or to the people around you, then it might be time for a style update! You don't have to go to great expense and purchase the latest fashion trends, because great looking style happens anywhere and can be found at all price points. Take stock of people around you who you feel speak to your aesthetic, how would you describe their look? Colorful? Playful? Pretty and polished? Rugged?

36. **Stop Monitoring:** It might be counterintuitive, but the number one was you can successfully and quickly achieve your goals is to let go of their outcome. When you put pressure on yourself to "be happy" or to "get

going" or to not think negatively, you end up thinking of that very thing. The human brain is wired to focus on the very thing that you are trying to avoid. There are values to all human emotions, and to relentlessly pursue a few, such as joy and happiness, while ignoring others, like sadness, is denying the warning signals of these emotions.

37. **It's all in Your Head:** Remember how annoyed you were when you were stuck in traffic the other day, which made you late for the event that you absolutely had to attend. You felt so angry that you were sweating and utterly exasperated when you arrived almost 30 minutes late. It would be easy to link the source of your irritation to the traffic delay, but when you think about it rationally, you are angry at the idea of being late. You felt negatively because it is your belief in the value of punctuality. To make this subtle shift is freeing---you should now realize that most everything you judge objectively as good or bad, can be modulated in your mind—through your approach and beliefs that you hold.

38. **Meditate:** It is important to find time to reflect in stillness. The ancient practice of sitting meditation (sitting still, focusing on one's breath, gently redirecting to the breath, and letting thoughts move in and out of your consciousness). This redirection toward finding stillness within ourselves is enhanced by the next tip #39 where ego is put in its place.

39. **Take Down Ego:** Here the term "ego" is not merely a description of the part of the human experience which is arrogant, but rather the notion of one's own "false self." It is the voice inside your mind that criticizes,

doubts, and is entirely judgmental of you and others. Taking down ego is challenging because the ego always tries to justify its existence. Meditation and stillness (or prayer) can help redirect the ego and quiet it down.

40. **Vibrate High:** Recall from the previous chapter the idea that all the universe is made up of energy which vibrates and emanates forward at different frequencies. Over time similar energies are drawn together---"like attracts like" and therefore, it is imperative to exude a high, that is, positive sense of energy in order to received that from the universe.

41. **Just Do:** One of the biggest misconceptions in the self-help industry is the notion that you must feel good all the time in order to be successful, happy, or productive. This is simply not the case. Too many people make the mistake of believing that they must overcome their feelings of procrastination in order to become productive---but in reality, you don't need to feel any particular feeling to get started in what you are doing. You can simply start. And it is this false belief that one must feel motivated to begin, when in reality, your feelings are fleeting and may not reflect the real truth of the matter, which is that your thoughts are not who you are...but they can become things in the real world.

42. **Be Shortsighted:** While you have now in your possession, a short list of goals that you are working toward accomplishing, once in a while, it is helpful to train your focus away from creating strict goals and objectives and instead focus on whatever you can accomplish at hand. It is similar to being a "home cook" versus being a chef. The chef may have designed dishes meticulously in their mind, and then setting about to

find and put together those dishes. However, a home cook simply looks around at what he or she has available. Referring to the goal of having a happier marriage, you may have the goal of taking your spouse out to a fancy dinner every week, or you may simply decide to create a romantic outing closer to home---the end goal still gets you closer to your vision of a more satisfying relationship.

43. **Be Insecure:** Nothing lasts forever. This is a fact. People and animals grow old and die, buildings break down, cars stop running---this is the way of the world to devolve into chaos. However, we do not accept this, the human impulse is to create extra security around ourselves---we frantically waste energy by running around making sure all the doors are locked to the point where we are scared more often than not. What if we exercised prudence (lock the door) without fear? To do so means that we have to accept the impermanence of all things. If we did this, most likely we will become free.

44. **Be Open:** Many times, once we have our goals in hand, many people charge off in pursuit of them, without ever returning to re-evaluate them. But to be vulnerable, to be open to what the universe tells us to do, even when the signal is to give up on the goal requires a willingness to be open to any and all messages surrounding us. If you are charging hard toward a goal, but nothing seems to be changing or working, stop for a moment to consider what this means from the standpoint of the universe.

45. **Fail Often:** Our society places such a premium on success, that we rarely acknowledge failure, even

though failure is truly the best teacher. Think about this, when you first learn to play an instrument, the majority of the notes you struck were wring notes. But each and every time you struck a wrong note, what happened? You stopped playing, went back to correct the note, and then moved on. You can only ever learn to play and instrument when you make the wrong notes. And if you are given permission to fail, you can learn without fear---failure, in this case, is freedom.

46. **Be Helpful:** One of the best ways to coach yourself is to help others. It is extremely easy to get so involved in your own self-improvement plan that, in a strange way, your ego becomes strengthened by your own well-intentioned pursuit of success. Aside from meditation (which allows you to minimize the tyranny of your thoughts by having you see them as temporary and not who you are), the best way to get out of your own way is to volunteer to help others who are in need. So, find your local community centers and see how you too can become active. You'll find that *you will be helped* in a much deeper capacity than even the people that you helped.

47. **Be Grateful:** In a similar vein to tip #46, you want to be able to get out of your own head (away from your ego) by realizing on a daily basis, the remarkable gifts that you are receiving on a daily basis. Beyond "counting your blessings" with the obviously amazing things in your life such as your family---but something as simple as your favorite brand of coffee, or the fact that the weather is nice. These are miniscule things that make your life better, why not appreciate them? If you are grateful for the small things, you will find the big things will be gifted to you.

48. **Do Everything with Awareness:** This last tip for coaching yourself involves creating awareness as you engage in each and every task. If you are writing an email, pay all your attention to that email. Honor the recipient in your mind. If you are washing dishes, think about the sensation of the water and soap, and be grateful for the meal that was on the dish right beforehand. Anything and everything can be transformed into a pure moment of reflection and bliss if you choose it to be so. And living with this kind of awareness will enhance every aspect of your life.

CHAPTER 4

Coaching Your Clients / 54 Tips on Coaching Your Clients

This last chapter is devoted to your clients. We will focus on 54 tried and true strategies for pointing your coaching clients toward taking actions that will improve their health, get their schedules organized, make time for family, excel in their careers, and create the lasting loving types of relationships they desire most. Being a leader yourself, you are well equipped to help others take the lead in their own lives.

Up until now, you have focused on strategies that are focused on enhancing your life, but when working to coach others in leadership, there are several guidelines to keep in mind. Below, you will see how these guidelines are so significant because up until now, as you have worked on coaching only yourself, that it is not always easy to take a step back and become objective about someone else's life.

But not to worry, you will see in this chapter that many of those tips for enhanced leadership that have been introduced earlier can be very easily modified to better apply them to potential clients, employees, or any others that need and would welcome your help. In order to better pivot yourself from a "me" orientation to a "them" orientation is to keep the following principles in mind:

First, get to know 3 things at the outset about your coaching client: 1) Their overall vision of what they would like their lives to be. This list should be highly descriptive of the exact kind of life they would want. 2) The most important people in their lives. And 3) What they want to immediately change about their environment.

- **The vison board**: which we introduced in chapter 1, and put to good use in chapter 2, will be a good starting point to talk to your coaching client about what they envision for your future. You should get to know their board as a window into their dreams. Is there a big, beautiful new house right in the middle of the board? Is it surrounded by lovingly tended vegetable gardens and pictures of adorable dogs? Then, you'll know that they are looking to build a loving home base and tip #41 "just do" can be suggested with regards to getting them to go to a series of open houses in neighborhoods they live in to take tours of their dream homes. Knowing what your client really, truly desires in their life can make all their difference for giving them just the right advice at the right time.

- **The support group:** some of the most important people in your client's life are very likely the biggest reasons why your client wants to change their lives for the better. Are they wanting to get healthy and lose weight so they can look and feel great for their spouse? Do they want more energy to play with their children? Having knowledge of who the client considers their inner circle of friends gamily directs you toward understanding the client's motivations for change, as well as additional, valuable insight on how to leverage their help. For example, in pursuit of their goal to learn to play the saxophone, you can call on your client's spouse to keep an eye on their practice week by week—your client now has a village of those who love and support them.

- **First things first:** What do they want to immediately change about their environment? Having your client name the most urgent stressors in their life can save you time and energy when it comes to coaching. Knowing that they absolutely hate their job is a clear signal to prioritize the vision of working at a job they absolutely love, rather than their less urgent goal of learning Spanish or planting an herb garden. It is like surveying your kitchen, taking stock of your recipes, and seeing the potential to create all these delicious dishes---none of which can taste very good, or even be made, when in fact, your stove is on fire! So, identify the things in your client's life that is "one fire" so that you can both focus your resources, and tailor your best leadership tips for these critical projects.

Now that you have some guidance on what to consider in general before plunging in to coaching your client, here are 50 strategies to apply in helping others reach their full potential. Some of these techniques are quick and easy, others are more involved, some will apply for many situations, others are much more specialized. Mix and match as you go along, relying on your intuition about what works best for different people.

49. **Know Their Vision:** By now, you should not only be able to recite your vision for exactly what you want, but you should know theirs as well.

50. **Know Their Strengths:** Every person has qualities that are definite assets, ask them what they think these are. Are they resilient? Do you practice great listening skills? Are they intensely creative? Assess these strengths for yourself---do you see them in the person? Rethink this list, what strengths do you perceive of them that they themselves do not see as strengths.

When they meet the inevitable challenges in pursuing their goals, this list be come in handy.

51. **Know Their Weaknesses:** Just as important as knowing strengths, to know their weaknesses opens a window to your client's core, so you better understand how to help them, and to perhaps using the instances when they stumble in their weaknesses as coaching moments.

52. **Remind Them it's a Process:** When times get tough, tell them that "It doesn't matter where you start but where you end up." This will put mistakes and the inevitable missteps into perspective.

53. **Ask Them "What's the Worst That Can Happen?":** Sometimes clients will stagnate because they have an unformed fear about a worst case scenario---challenge them on this and ask them to fully explore what would happen if the absolute "worst thing" comes to pass. This exercise helps empower them in two ways, first they can see the unlikelihood of that very thing actually happening, and two they will appreciate how quickly they are able to come up with solutions and/or face the consequences.

54. **Encourage Sleep:** Strangely enough, an effective way to help your client is to get them to sleep more. While it may be tougher to push healthy exercise and eating (clients know these things already and these changes are difficult to implement fully), gently nudging them to go to bed earlier and earlier is much easier than you think, and reaps a world of benefits.

55. **Check in Often:** Connection is key, keep in touch at least once a day via text, email, or ideally a phone call. Even a 5-minute conversation can help someone feel cared for and is encouraging.

56. **Get Personal:** Your client has a private life of course, but when it is appropriate, make sure you check in on them that there are not major family, career, or social stressors that are weighing them down. For the amount they are comfortable enough to share, get to know your client's needs this way.

57. **Less Bad News:** It's important to know what is going in the world, but with the abundance of world-wide media coverage, it is vital to encourage your client to consume this material just enough to be informed, but not to flood yourself with negative imagery every day.

58. **More Good News:** On the flip side of tip #57---find more good news to share. Find media stories of good news and read them, send funny video clips to share.

59. **Create Rituals:** Put aside time to pour a hot cup of tea or coffee, or take a slow walk, or read a poem. A small, purely pleasurable ritual will create a sense of ceremony and space to breath every day.

60. **Write Your Vision by Hand:** Every day we are constantly on our phones and laptops. Rarely do we jot much down---but there is something special about writing something by hand, so encourage your client to journal, even if it is only for a few minutes, by hand each day, reflecting on or reaffirming their vision.

61. **Go One Level Up:** As your client makes progress, it is important to keep a steady pace of improvement that hits the balancing point between being challenging but also within a reasonable reach---a "stretch reach" Ask them to describe the next concrete level they can pursue. This agreement on the doable next step will keep the momentum going.

62. **Ask one question every day:** Challenge your client by asking one provocative question every day, such as "What is the most valuable thing you own---and what would you trade it for?"

63. **Make One Contact:** To facilitate creating a network that supports your client's goals, ask them to reach out to one person a day that is associated with their goals. It can be someone they already know, but the idea is to move them forward on their projects by getting them to make contact.

64. **Give A Sincere Compliment:** One, well-crafted and thoughtful compliment a day reminds them they are special.

65. **Help Them Reframe:** When a client gets stuck on interpreting a situation in a negative way, ask them, "What else could that mean?" and wait for 5 replies. Push them on this and they are reminded that situations have multiple meanings. Therefore, they can choose a better understanding of the situation.

66. **A Token:** A token is a small item that you can carry around with you that has significant meaning. Ask your client to choose a small item (a pebble, a shell, a chess

piece etc.) give it a meaning, and have them carry it around as a reminder of a valuable lesson.

67. **Smile:** It works to lift your spirit every time.

68. **Go for a Walk:** Like tip #67 this is an instant spirit lifter. Being out and about in nature will lighten your mood.

69. **Be Playful:** Get up from your desk and twirl around, sing out loud a silly song, do something to switch up the mood---it will remind you of how silly life can be.

70. **Be Biased Toward Action:** It is very easy to become bogged down with planning things down to the smallest details, free yourself from this trap by always "doing" something rather than only thinking it.

71. **Make a Game Plan:** Having stated the wisdom of tip #70...you and your client should have a plan of action. It can be something simple shared between the two of you, but it should be an organized plan of attack.

72. **Get an App:** Smart phones are now not only ubiquitous, but have powerful software and interfaces to keep track of your goals, productivity, and connectivity with a network of likeminded others.

73. **Power Breakfasting:** Plan out your day's objectives while eating a healthy breakfast—this creates the sense of ritual and ceremony (tip #59) as well as draws on the usefulness of a game plan (tip #71).

74. **Meet Your Client's Significant Others:** If you really want to help someone achieve their potential, you must get to know the most important person in their

life. Set up a meeting, you'll find this contact very important for many reasons.

75. **Have Homework:** Write down one thing that will help your client achieve their goal that they can accomplish overnight.

76. **Take on One of their Goals:** Maybe if their goal is to lose 5 pounds, why not buddy up with them and do the same thing…it will give you both perspective and provides them with support.

77. **Build in a Break:** At times, when the going gets too tough, tell your client that it is okay to walk away. For those of us who are rebels at heart, or who love to question the world, it is actually beneficial to have the option that it's possible to quit, stop, or pause. When we are told "no" our souls can push back against being pushed down. Remember that you don't have to stop, just like you don't have to keep going---but simply having the option to quit is often all that is needed for you or the client to keep going.

78. **Commit Publically:** If your client is trying to achieve a goal that would benefit from crowd sourced support---suggest they promote it on social media. Without being obnoxious about it, sharing your intentions with a supportive and fun group of friends can be expand your help by several fold, and magnifies the support they receive.

79. **Travel Somewhere:** Even if it is an overnight stay in the next city over, suggest to your client that they get out of town. This gesture of symbolically "getting out of their rut" will impart a sense of importance and

ceremony around their life dreams and goals. Have them travel someplace new to reflect upon their vision as needed when the time comes for a fresher perspective.

80. **Simplify:** This tip was reflected in the tips for high level self-coaching, but should definitely be applied to your client---have them pare down their belongings on a regular basis to things they love and enjoy. This clarifies their life as well as their goals.

81. **Let the Mind Wander:** Some of the most creative solutions occur when you are window shopping, doodling, taking a shower, or taking a long walk. It is during routines that require very little attention that we often let down our guard. When you or your client are bogged down, or even when you've worked at length on a project, allow the mind to roam free. You may be surprised at what happens.

82. **Making a Chain:** If productivity is part of their vision (such as writing a novel, or running a marathon), have them record their progress in a symbolic way---such as dropping coins in a vase or stringing beads on a string—the visual representation will keep them moving along.

83. **Hand Hold on One Thing:** If you find that your client has hit a slump, ask them to name one small thing—the absolute smallest task they can accomplish that day and then ask them to do it in front of you. You can for example say, "Make that phone call now, I'll wait." This may seem like a parental gesture, but this small gesture of concern is often enough to get people moving over a bumpy spot.

84. **Make Them "Disappear":** Get your client to free up more time for themselves by having them say "no" to volunteering for people or projects that they do not want to do, but feel pressured to complete because of the expectations of others. Remind your client that they should only complete projects that they are currently passionate about. This permission to say no makes them less available to time and energy vampires (these include people as well as ill-advised projects).

85. **The Stop-List:** In a similar vein to tip #84, have your client write down all the things they want to stop doing. This list should include events and projects that are no longer fun, necessary, and/or appealing. Have your client write them down, briefly describe what they are, and then have them tear up the paper. It is liberating to not be burdened by doing things that are not of value to you anymore.

86. **Work in Cycles:** A key productivity issue is exhaustion. But you can often short circuit the system of mental fatigue by working only in increments of 25-90 minutes and taking a break (5 minutes to 30 minutes). This stop and start will allow time for rest and spacing so that you can continue working throughout the day.

87. **Remember The Best:** Having a keystone memory will be encouraging for your client when things feel helpless or have hit a standstill. Have them tell you about a key peak moment when they felt great peace or success so that they may embody these sensations.

88. **It is Only Now:** Remember that in whatever capacity you are working, you only have the moment that you

are currently inhabiting as the key moment where anything works. The past is gone and the future is theoretical. Bring your client back to the moment if you find them lost in either looking forward or backward.

89. **Power Snack:** It's a small thing, but have your client create a power snack that is healthy and tasty. And then, whenever things slow down or they hit a slump, they can circle back to take a break and have their power snack...somehow it is reassuring and feels comforting.

90. **Take on an Offbeat Creative Hobby:** If they have never ever wanted to learn to crochet, or tap dance, or raise orchids, gently challenge them to do something outside their comfort zone. Taking on a new hobby tilts their perspective, especially if that hobby has never occurred to them before.

91. **Write a Love Letter:** Have your client write a meaningful letter to someone who has been important in their life. Very few people write letters anymore, but the act of creating a grateful and meaningful letter will remind your client of their great fortune to be loved.

92. **Treasure The Failures:** When a client hits a setback, have them write down one past failure in detail and then describe 3 things they learned from that event as well as 1 major thing that became better because of what they learned. This will put their "failure" in perspective.

93. **Mini Vision Board:** We've already talked about making a vision board, but making a smaller, more portable version serves as an exciting reminder of what

they really want. Ideas for what they can do is to create the board online, or use a regular sized piece of typing paper instead of a big poster board.

94. **Master the Music Game:** Make a playlist of productivity music and play it every single day. Your mind and body will become instantly attuned to begin working as soon as you hear the first notes on the first song, it will become automatic.

95. **One Song Wonder:** In keeping with tip #94 (mastering the music game), ask your client to choose one particular song that really rocks them out---that they love it so much that it instantly gets their heart racing and their body moving. This will be their anthem. They can play this song whenever they need to be "pumped up" before a big meeting, event, or just to get to work.

96. **Name One Person**: Sometimes, despite our best efforts, we truly falter in pursuit of our goals. A times like these, we just don't see the point of working harder, so we are willing to put off our efforts or even quit. If your client is at this crossroads, have them think about one person that would really benefit from them achieving their goal, and have them visualize that person as the recipient of these benefits. For example, if the goal is to lose weight and become healthier, ask the client to think of their spouse or child, who would gain a great deal from this goal (they have a healthier spouse or parents). Most times, we are willing to do things for people we love more so than ourselves.

97. **Be of Service**: Volunteering for a good cause gets your client involved in the city or neighborhood you live in

by agreeing to help tutor an at-risk high school student, spend time with those less fortunate, are all things that bring high value to not only the person involved, but to an entire community.

98. **Name What is Under Your Control:** Sometimes, a client will feel so overwhelmed that they do not realize that they have much more control over the situation than they do---and many times, that control begins with their own actions. Have them make a list of things they are currently able to control in that moment; it will bring clarity to a stressful situation.

99. **Name What is NOT Under Your Control:** By the same token, have them write down the list of things that they cannot control. It will also be counter-balance to the above listing of things that they are in charge of. By differentiating what you are able to control from what you are not, creates precision in your plans and objectives.

Finally, the last two tips for successful coaching involve taking the perspective that leadership coaching is a dynamic, sometimes exhausting, many times exhilarating, but always worthwhile journey that anyone can take. Make the most of your life by becoming a leader.

Always remember:

100. **It's Another Day:** The way we handle setbacks is often more important than how many successes we accumulate. Have your client describe how they will handle a disappointing situation by drawing on strategies they have employed in the past. Also, walk with them through different scenarios where they can

apply those strategies to any current disappointment. This will serve to remind them of their resilience and provide a game plan for how to effectively approach setbacks next time.

101. **Be a Role Model:** Create a life that you love and your client will always have a model to emulate. Your life and how you lead it is the greatest and most instructive inspiration for those around you.

CONCLUSION

Putting it All Together /

Creating Visionary Leadership

'I feel that a great coach is one that has a vision, sets a plan in place has the right people in place to execute that plan and then accepts the responsibility if that plan is not carried out."

Mike Singletary

Congratulations! You are well on your way to becoming a world class leader in the parts of your life that you have decided are the most important. No one can ever take away this vision of who you are at your best self.

By now, you have seen that the path to becoming a great leader or coach can happen in many different ways, in fact, a 101 pathways. But what brings all this great variety together, how do you make your choices between suggesting your client tip #73, power breakfasting (where you make your plans of the day through the morning ritual of eating a good and health breakfast), or the power tip #68, power walking (using your walking time or morning run routine to prepare for your day as well). Well, it all depends on the schedule and temperament of the client, which are both types of information that a good coach would either know already, or certainly get to know of their client. In this case, questions you should ask are:

- ☐ Is it possible my coaching client can perform both tips and modify them so that ding both can make sense and impart high value? Perhaps they can perform their power run *and* then have the power breakfast. During both times they can create and reflect on their various to-do lists, or hone in on the "one" (or 2-3) things that they must accomplish that day. If they only have time and/or energy for one of the power tips in the morning, then the next step is to ask the follow-up questions that determine what are the most important priorities in the household:

- What are the other significant influences in the client's life that would narrow down the choice? For example, if your client has a family, especially one with small children, then the inclination is that the client will want to spend time with their children during breakfast, at which time, the power breakfast rule of planning out your day may be distracted by the joy/horror of having breakfast with a toddler—they simply can't concentrate at that time. On the other hand, maybe they have older children who may relish the opportunity to have their parent talk to them about their plans for the day. This can be a bonding experience when a mom or dad says to their kid, "Hey, I need to get this thing done today, and it takes these different steps. Which thing should I do first and why do you think this?" Your child will be so surprised that you would seek their insight and share your personal decision making that they will likely offer an interesting insight or suggestion. Try it, see if it works.

As you can see, there is no straightforward or blind application of every coaching strategy. There are no one size fits all principles. In the absence of universal rules, coaching becomes something of an art form, and you must be flexible to better serve your client.

Another important takeaway point of this book is the following: you alone get to decide. While in this book, we have talked a lot about the importance of your inner circle of family and friends. We have called them your co-coaches or your assistance coaches because they are your partners in better decision making, quite simply, you can't nor should you even try to go at it all alone. Further, you need not only their help and insight, but you need to consult them. But no matter how much your life's objectives are entwined with another person, you alone get to decide. It can be incredibly easy to forget this distinction, especially when your goal or objective is tied up seamlessly with someone else.

For example, many people reading this book, wish for a passionate, romantic, and inspiring relationship with their spouse or significant other. This may seem like a dream that involves the input of two people---and in many ways it is. You simply can't be the sole partner in a partnership. However, you will quickly realize that beyond providing this other person a loving and compassionate presence and hoping this will influence them, you cannot make someone else do anything.

You are the only person in control of your decisions, and you alone get to decide. This realization may be frightening, but it can also impart a sense of freedom---you get to do whatever you want. So, while it is vital to beam only the most loving positive energy to those around you and the ones you cherish most in your life, know that you can only affect your desires and dreams through your own actions. Your leadership behavior is your own, so...own it!

Finally, with so many great techniques to better focus and train your mind, there is no doubt that you can feel overwhelmed, turned around, or otherwise confused by what your next steps will be, but the one final truth of being an extraordinary leaders and coach remains: it all starts with your vision.

In the day to day living of your routines, it's easy to either get caught up in unexpected chaos (a flat tire on the way to work, a suddenly sick child at home, a forgotten meeting at work), or to lose yourself in the monotony (same lunch each day, same drive home etc.). The key to staying focused in the midst of the latest mini-crisis, or to try and break out of a ho-hum and boring routine is to consult your visionary goals (tip #1). What are your objectives? What are your wildest dreams? To keep those in mind will be your anchor when all is going awry in your schedule, or your kick starter when your engine has slowed down considerably. When you go back again and again to your visions, you'll see how easy it is to choose just the right strategy, just the perfect principle, and the most terrific tip to coach yourself or someone else to a better life.

Best of luck on what will surely be a fantastic journey into joyful leadership!

BOOK RECOMMENDATION

Coaching Questions

101 Coaching Questions for the Coach and the Coaching Client for an Empowering Coaching Session

by Randy Wayne

AVAILABLE NOW ON AMAZON.COM

JULY 2016

www.ingramcontent.com/pod-product-compliance
Lightning Source LLC
Chambersburg PA
CBHW021443170526
45164CB00001B/362